How Artists Use

Line and Tone

Paul Flux

Heinemann
LIBRARY

H www.heinemann.co.uk
Visit our website to find out more information about Heinemann Library books.

To order:
☎ Phone 44 (0) 1865 888066
▤ Send a fax to 44 (0) 1865 314091
▢ Visit the Heinemann Bookshop at www.heinemann.co.uk to browse our catalogue and order online.

First published in Great Britain by Heinemann Library, Halley Court, Jordan Hill, Oxford OX2 8EJ, a division of Reed Educational and Professional Publishing Ltd.
Heinemann is a registered trademark of Reed Educational & Professional Publishing Ltd.

OXFORD MELBOURNE AUCKLAND JOHANNESBURG BLANTYRE
GABORONE IBADAN PORTSMOUTH (NH) USA CHICAGO

Designed by Celia Floyd
Illustrations by Jo Brooker/Ann Miller
Originated by Ambassador Litho Ltd.
Printed and bound in Hong Kong/China

05 04 03 02 01
10 9 8 7 6 5 4 3 2 1
ISBN 0 431 11524 9

British Library Cataloguing in Publication Data

Flux, Paul
  How artists use line and tone.
  1.Line (Art) – Juvenile literature 2.Shades and shadows (Art) – Juvenile literature
  I.Title
  741

Acknowledgements
The Publishers would like to thank the following for permission to reproduce photographs:
Aachen: Neue Galerie-Sammlung Ludwig/© The Estate of Roy Lichtenstein/DACS 2001 p21; AKG, London: /© ADAGP, Paris, and DACS, London 2001 p20, /© DACS 2001 p7, /© Succession Picasso/DACS 2001 pp8, 9; Albright Knox Art Gallery, Buffalo, New York/Bridgeman Art/DACS 2001: p17; Australian National Gallery/Bridgeman/© ARS, NY and DACS 2001: p24; Carnegie Museum of Art, Pittsburgh; Fellows Fund, Women's Committee Acquisition Fund, and Patrons Art Fund/© Kate Rothko Prizel and Christopher Rothko/DACS 2001: p28; Corbis: Archivo Iconografico, SA p12, National Gallery, London p10; Mary Evans Picture Library: p18; Musée d'Orsay, Paris/AKG, London: p15; Royal Albert Museum, Exeter, Devon/Bridgeman Art Library: p16; SCALA/© ADAGP, Paris and DACS, London 2001: p5; St Bride Printing Library: p19; Tate, London 2000: p13, Henry Moore Foundation p14; The Cleveland Museum of Art, John L. Severance Fund, 1971.136: p27; Trevor Clifford: p25; V & A Picture Library: p11.

Cover photograph reproduced with permission of Aachen: Neue Galerie-Sammling Ludwig/© The Estate of Roy Lichtenstein/DACS 2001.

Every effort has been made to contact copyright holders of any material reproduced in this book. Any omissions will be rectified in subsequent printings if notice is given to the Publisher.

Contents

What can a line do?   4

Lines are not all the same   6

Lines can have meaning   8

How lines make space   10

Lines old and new   12

An artist's view of the modern world   14

Pictures that seem to move   16

Just black and white   18

Lines work in many ways   20

Take a line for a walk   22

Different tools and techniques   24

How to draw a face using line   26

Tones and feelings   28

Glossary   30

Index   32

Any words appearing in the text in bold, **like this**, are explained in the Glossary.

What can a line do?

A line is a simple mark on paper. Some are straight, others are curved, wavy and zigzag! A line can do many things. A line can make shapes in a picture, it can **divide** space and it can even carry feelings. When more than one line is drawn, patterns and shapes are made. Look at these lines. What can you see?

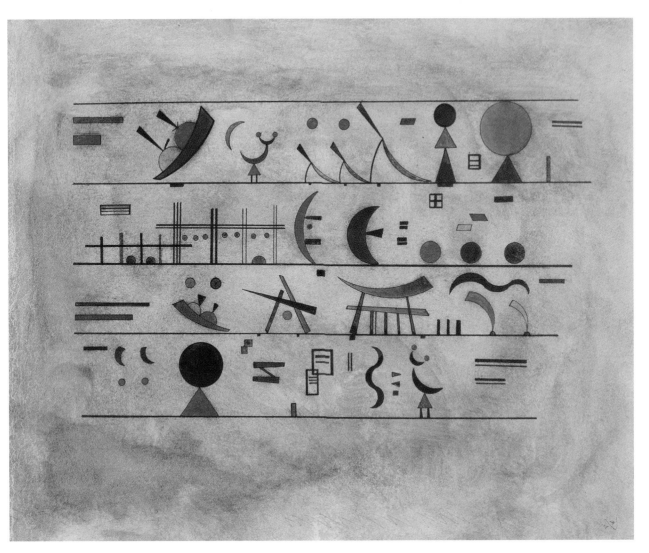

Wassily Kandinsky, *Lines of Signs*, 1931

In this picture you can see many lines. The five long ones are like a page of writing or music. The lines break up the space. Together they make shapes that could be part of an ancient language. The brown background makes the picture look like the wall of a tomb of a king who lived long ago. Can you see some common shapes, like circles, triangles and the moon?

Lines are not all the Same

Artists make lines in many different ways. Can you match these lines to the tools which made them? These lines show you some of the different kinds of lines there are. Some are thick, some are thin. Taken together they make a complete picture. Can you think of a good title for it? How about 'Thunderstorm'?

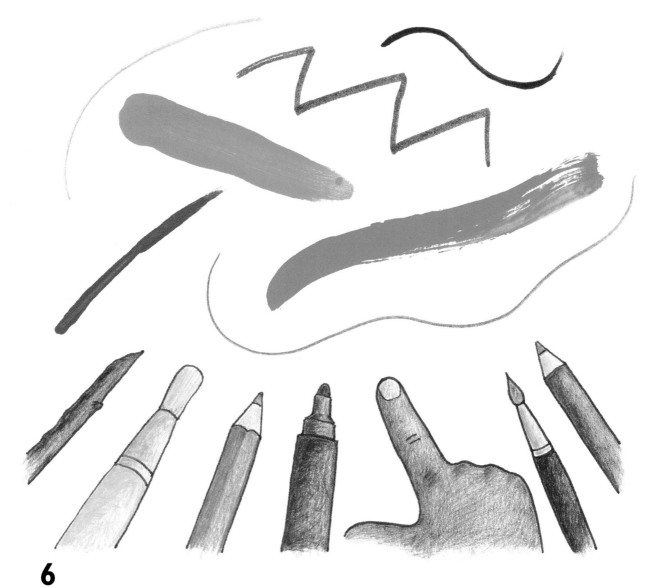

6

Paul Klee, *Scenery with Setting Sun,* 1919

Lines enclose a space, and they also help us recognize objects. The sun in this painting is clear, but look around the rest of the picture. Can you see how a house has been suggested by just a few lines? There are many spaces filled with different colour **tones**. Notice how the softer **shades** of blue and green make the orange sun even stronger. Is the dark arrow pulling the sun down?

Lines can have meaning

Pablo Picasso painted this famous picture in 1937, after German aircraft had bombed the beautiful Spanish city of Guernica. He wanted to show how terrible war can be. Picasso has used lines to make the shapes of animals and people. He has **shaded** these shapes to give black, grey and white **tones**. The people and animals have no colour but the grey and black still make a **dramatic** picture.

Pablo Picasso, *Guernica*, 1937

Here we see part of the painting in more detail. Look at how the woman's arms and face stand out against the dark background. Her hands are twisted as if she is in pain, or very angry. What do you think she might be saying? What is she feeling?

Detail from *Guernica*

How lines make Space

The **canvas** on which this picture is painted is perfectly flat, but the road seems to disappear far into the distance. Artists can use line to give pictures **depth**. We call this **perspective**. The artist has used a **vanishing point** to which our eye is drawn. Can you see where it is? It is where the road disappears from view.

Meindert Hobbema, *The Avenue at Middelharnis*, 1689

Here we can see the use of perspective in a picture of a town. This is Tokyo, Japan, about 150 years ago. Can you find the vanishing point? If you run your finger along the lines of the street you will find it. Look at how the people at the front of the picture are bigger – the smaller they are, the further away they must be.

Ando Hiroshige, *Saruwaka Cho Street*, 1856

Lines old and new

This is one of the first pictures ever made. It was painted on the wall of a cave and could be more than 20,000 years old! It shows some stick-like men hunting deer. The artist has used lines to show the shape of the deer and then filled in the space with colour. The artist drew the deer very carefully, but did not try so hard with the people because they were not so important in the picture.

**Cave painting,
Spain**

Alfred Wallis, *The Blue Ship*, about 1934

Alfred Wallis was a painter who lived in Cornwall, England. He only started painting when he was 68 years old. He painted **scenes** of sailing ships. He did not try to make this picture look real. The lighthouses are small because the ship is the most important object in the picture. The thick lines of the ship, and the **solid** colours, give the feeling of movement at sea.

An artist's view of the modern world

Henry Moore,
Tube Shelter Perspective,
1941

Henry Moore was an English artist most famous for his **sculpture.** During World War II (1939–45) he drew this picture of people sheltering from the terrible bombing in London. The lines of huddled people mix with the lines of the tunnel to make it feel like they are trapped. The grey, white and yellow **tones** work together to make the people seem like insects wrapped up in **cocoons.**

14

Do you think washing makes a good **subject** for a picture? The French artist Edgar Degas liked to paint and draw **scenes** from everyday life. He thought that the modern world was a good subject for his pictures. Here we see two women ironing. Their bodies are straining with the effort of the hard work. The bold lines and dull colour tones make an ordinary action seem special.

Edgar Degas, *Women Ironing*, 1884

Pictures that Seem to move

Here we see a fine sailing ship fighting against a terrible storm. The sails are torn and, although we can't see any people, we can sense the panic they must be feeling. The rocks on the right are black and frightening. George Reinagle has balanced the **delicate** lines of the moving ship with the dark **tones** of the sky and waves. How would you feel if you were on this ship?

George Reinagle, *A First Rate Man-of-War*, about 1826

Giacomo Balla, *Dynamism of a Dog on a Leash*, 1912

Almost 100 years ago, a group of artists called the
Futurists decided they could show the modern world
through painting movement and speed. This picture looks
like a **scene** from a film. The dog and its owner are rushing
past us. The lines of the background mix with the dark
colour to make the picture look full of sudden movement.

Just black and white

Gustave Doré, Illustration for Dante's book *The Divine Comedy*, **about 1861**

Gustave Doré was a popular book **illustrator** in 19th-century England. His pictures were etched (cut) onto metal plates and then printed. A deep cut on the metal gives a dark **tone**. Can you see the rocks, the sea, the cliff and the sky? No colour has been used, only line. The **shaded** tones are made by different thicknesses of line. How do you think these people feel?

18

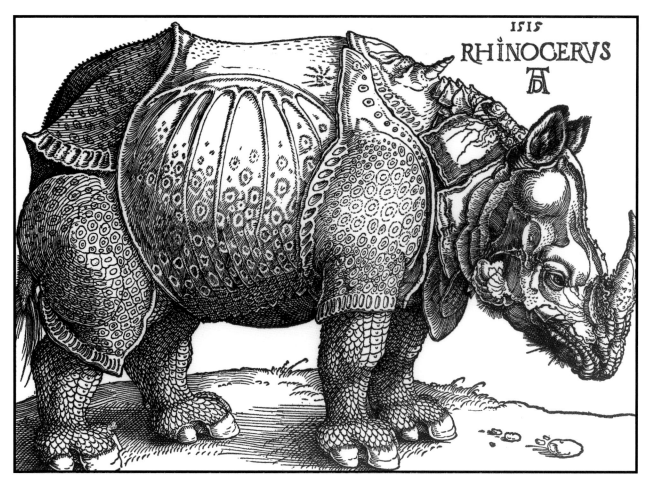

Albrecht Dürer, *Rhinoceros*, 1515

This is an **engraving** by the German artist Albrecht Dürer. Can you see the date and how he signed the picture with his initials? The artist has used just line and shade to give the animal its shape. The patterns of the skin are highly **decorative**, and make the rhinoceros look **armour-plated**. When this picture was made, few people had ever seen a rhinoceros. Do you think Dürer had?

Lines work in many ways

This picture seems to be bursting out of the centre of the page and yet it is perfectly flat! The artist has used his **skill** with line to make this happen. There is a perfect circle in the centre. Can you see the four lines of oval shapes? These run across the picture like a giant cross and draw your eye to the middle. The bright **tones** at the centre look brighter because of the duller **shades** at the edge.

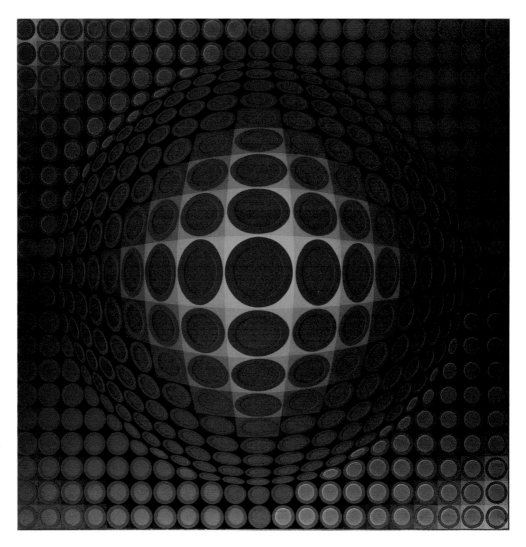

Victor Vasarely, *Vega 200,* 1968

**Roy Lichtenstein,
*Still Life with
Lemons,* 1975**

Lines can work together to have a **dramatic** effect. In this picture Roy Lichtenstein has used dark lines to break the picture into pieces. He has painted stripes of different colours which work together. Do you find that your eyes are drawn to the lemons in the middle of the picture? This is because their **solid** shape and bright tone is made stronger by the lines around them.

Take a line for a walk

Draw some lines across the paper. Think about making them straight or curvy, thick or thin. Should some lines make a pattern together? Can you see the **outline** of any shapes? Do you want to finish them? When you have drawn your lines think about **shade** and colour, and fill in some of the spaces. You have made an **abstract** picture! Now you can give it a title.

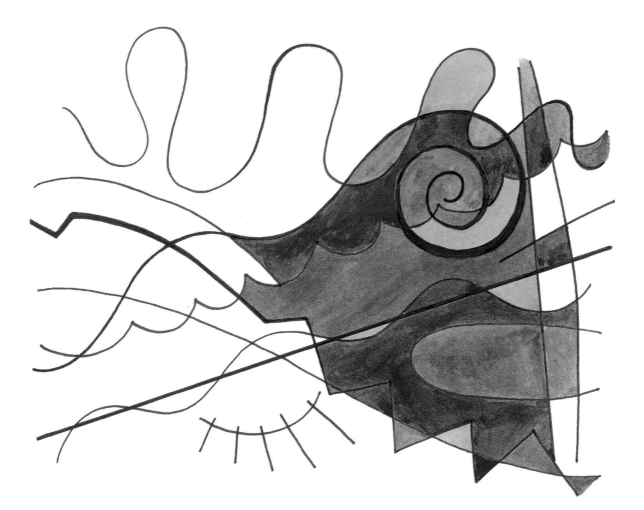

22

Paul Klee, the Swiss artist, said that 'drawing a line is like taking a dot for a walk'. Get a selection of tools and then try to draw as many different lines as you can. Can you draw lines for these words? Which colours will you use? Some are really difficult!

open   closed   fat   sad   hot   fast   angry
        calm   friendly   scared

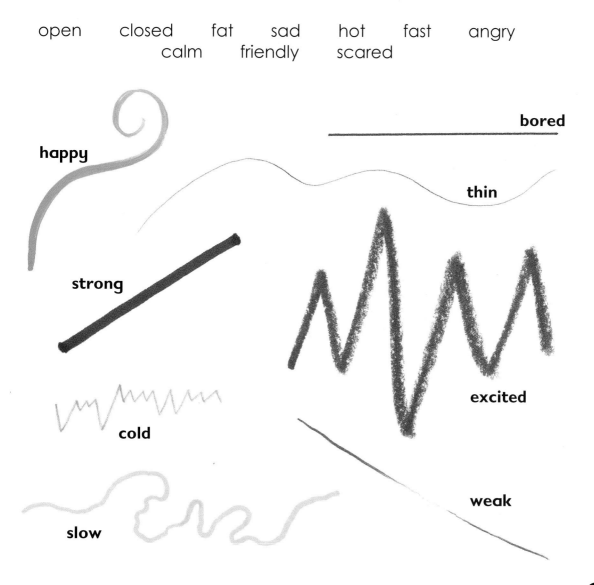

happy

bored

thin

strong

excited

cold

weak

slow

Different tools and techniques

Jackson Pollock, *Blue Poles*, 1952

Jackson Pollock found exciting ways of **applying** paint.
He flicked, dripped and splashed lines of paint onto glass
on the floor. When he had finished he gave the picture a
title which came from something he saw in the painting.
Can you see why he called this *Blue Poles*? What might
Jackson Pollock have been thinking about when he
painted this picture?

Lay lots of newspaper on the floor and get the largest
piece of paper you can find (A3, A2 or even A1!). Use
different brushes and paints and flick and drip colours
one at a time onto the paper. You could put some runny
paint into a plastic bag or pot, make a small hole in the
bottom and then swing it carefully over the paper. Don't
use too much paint and stop before you completely
cover the paper (and yourself!) in paint.

How to draw a face using line

Portraits have been painted from the very earliest times. This lovely portrait was made to go over the top of an Egyptian **mummy**, about 1900 years ago. The artist has used line, **tone** and **shadow** to bring out the beauty of the face. Look hard at her eyes. She cannot speak to us now, but can you sense her saying 'I was once alive like you'?

Portrait of a Woman, about AD **100**

Try drawing a portrait yourself. Start by getting someone to model for you. Sketch the **outline** of the face first, using a soft pencil. Lightly draw in the eyes, nose and mouth. Then use lines to create shadow to one side. When you have finished, use a harder pencil to highlight the outline and main features.

Mark Rothko, *Yellow, Blue on Orange*, 1955

The American artist Mark Rothko painted large pictures using blocks of colour. In each block he uses different colour **tones**. Can you see how the orange frame seems to be holding the other colours in? What do you think about when you look at this picture? Do you think you could paint something like this? You can!

1. Mix a colour, red or blue for example, and use this to cover all your paper. Let it dry completely.
2. Choose two different colours and mix each one into a **shade** you like. Don't use very dark colours.
3. Paint a fuzzy rectangle using one of the colours. Mix in small amounts of another colour to change the tones slightly. Repeat this with your second colour.

Try painting another picture using different colours and sizes of shape. This is just what Rothko did!

Glossary

abstract kind of art which does not try to show people or things, but instead uses shape and colour to make the picture

apply how paint is put onto a surface

armour-plated covered in armour, a metal which protects

canvas strong woven material on which many artists paint

cocoon silky case spun by some insects to protect themselves or their eggs

decorative pleasant or interesting to look at

delicate very fine, gentle

depth the feeling of space and distance in a picture

divide to split into two or more parts

dramatic something which is surprising or exciting

engraving picture made by cutting into something hard, like metal or wood

Futurists group of Italian painters working about 100 years ago

illustrator person who makes pictures for books

mummy dead body which has been treated with chemicals to make it last a long time

outline line which shows the edge and shape of an object

perspective the way an artist draws or paints on a flat surface, so that there seems to be space and distance in the picture

portrait painting which shows what someone looks like

scene view painted by an artist

sculpture three-dimensional art, usually made with wood, clay, stone or metal

shade a darker or lighter version of a colour

shadow shading caused when light is blocked out

skill ability to do something difficult really well

solid something which looks like a real, physical object

subject what a picture is about

tone shades and depth of colour, from light to dark or dull to bright

vanishing point place in a picture where all the lines of perspective meet and where the picture seems to disappear into the distance. Some pictures have more than one vanishing point.

Index

abstract art   22

Balla, Giacomo   17

cave painting   12

colour   7, 12, 13, 15, 17, 21, 22, 28, 29

Degas, Edgar   15

Doré, Gustave   18

dramatic effect   8, 21

Dürer, Albrecht   19

etching   18

feelings   4, 9, 16, 18, 19

Futurists   17

Hiroshige, Ando   11

Hobbema, Meindert   10

Kandinsky, Wassily   5

Klee, Paul   7

Lichtenstein, Roy   21

Moore, Henry   14

mummy   26

outlines   7, 22, 27

patterns   4, 22

perspective   10, 11

Picasso, Pablo   8, 9

Pollock, Jackson   24

portraits   26, 27

Reinagle, George   16

Rothko, Mark   28, 29

shade   8, 18, 19, 20, 22, 29

shadow   26, 27

shapes   4, 5, 7, 12, 20, 21, 28

solid colours   13

solid shapes   7, 21

techniques   24–5, 29

tools   6, 23, 25

vanishing point   10, 11

Vasarely, Victor   20

Wallis, Alfred   13